Nate and Kate

by David Hayes
illustrated by Faye Miller

Practice Decodable 14

Mc Graw Hill Education

Bothell, WA • Chicago, IL • Columbus, OH • New York, NY

MHEonline.com

Send all inquiries to:
McGraw-Hill Education
8787 Orion Place
Columbus, OH 43240

ISBN: 978-0-02-130455-4
MHID: 0-02-130455-6

Printed in China.

9 10 11 12 13 DSS 27 26 25 24 23

Nate made a sand hut.

A big wave came!

"Make a big sand hut!" said Kate.

"Can a wave hit that?" said Nate.

"Yes!"

"But that is fun!" said Kate.

Kate and Nate made a big hut.